VIGNETTES OF THE POSSIBLY DYING

KB ELIZA

Copyright © 2021 by KB Eliza All rights reserved

Ponderings Publications

No part of this book may be reproduced in any form or by any electronic or mechanical means, including information storage and retrieval systems, without written permission from the author or publisher.

WWW.KBELIZA.COM

FACEBOOK.COM/WRITERKBELIZAOFFICIAL

INSTAGRAM.COM/K.B.ELIZA

TWITTER.COM/KBELIZAOFFICIAL

TIKTOK KBELIZA

For Papa, I kept my promise x

PROLOGUE

There is no movement or sense of pathway between here and there. I open my eyes, kneeling on the grass. Outside? But this meant before now, I was inside asleep.

Which shade of green eludes me with this grass? The closest I can come to is a vivid high definition of shamrock, emerald, fern, parakeet and jade, every single blade luminous, defined soft and living, breathing. This is the closest.

My hand sits in it, and on it at the same time, I feel every separate piece like strands of fine silken hair. Light as dust, moving in gentle waves. So strange. It is the truest real I have never seen before, and yet part of me senses I have known it always, had I forgotten it existed? If only memory was music, perhaps I could write a symphony to show you. A riddle, it seems. I am a wordsmith, and yet I am a beggar hungry for words. Did God design a human brain that could not conceive of these shapes and dimensions?

. . .

LOVE FILLS ME, AND THERE IS A COMPLETE ABSENCE OF DARKNESS IN every cell of my body that ever was and will be. At this moment, all is connected and interwoven in a majestic, unfathomable, synchronistic pattern, reason and measurement that is finite and sharp, precise and without limit. A love is the prayer of a million mothers calling their children home, love that is the feeling of complete and unquestioned safety and chest-bursting ethereal omnipresence. Home. This is home; the realisation is joy unencumbered. The complete absence of dark, fear, anger, greed or any kind of violence.

NONE OF THIS HAS ANY CONCEPTUAL LANGUAGE TO DEFINE IN ANY accuracy.
Once a door opens so big and bright the blinding of it makes your heart thump. You look behind, and it causes tears to fall. Relief, heart- break, and restoration. You hold your humble gratitude like a huge and heavy star in your hands, and your knees wobble under the weight of it. This is not a normal day. You shall not ever have another normal day again. This is exceptional.

I had a choice, to stay or return in that moment. But there was fair warning. Because you cannot touch here without taking some of it back with you, which is difficult for the body to handle, it is the hardest journey to know all this beauty, and love, then go back to what you knew before. I was told you must to ask for help, and guidance will come. You are not alone; you are never alone.

When I returned, I woke and told everyone I had to write; there was so much. I received odd looks, which told me quickly, this was hard to fathom. Nevertheless, I wrote down all I could remember, the knowledge and understandings just as I promised.

The world felt flat, dark, full of fear and depression. Shapes were missing; it was as though I could push the air over like a cardboard cut-out. As though the world was a fake copy and behind the very air was the real place. How could I be here? How could I know what I know and not tell anyone? To tell the dying friend, you are not dying; you are beginning. It is not a heaven of imaginings and clouds; it is more real than here. It is physical. Things I thought were true before I knew were not; things I wanted to believe in were completely truer than I could have imagined. Some things we are not meant to know right now. Some memories have faded over time.

A slow process, I have learned to seek God out in the natural world, within and in the hearts of others. The beauty and appreciation of here, this palace of learning, has returned. I am finally able to find joy in being here. Escapism is a dreadful master. There were times I clutched at faded grass and begged to go back. I have been frightened to share, to find courage to say what I know. Our ego seeks to be understood and accepted, so fighting the ego to keep a promise is hard. The death of ego is the final frontier.

WRITE WHAT YOU HAVE BEEN SHOWN. SO I DID. THERE WILL BE consequences.

HEAVEN IS NOT A ZENITH. IT IS A PHYSICAL PLACE. THEY WERE RIGHT; you cannot touch it without bringing sand back on your feet. These moments are like coal and diamonds, sand and glass. Maybe you will find a jewel to keep for yourself and let it spark the torch you carry on this long dark night.

KB ELIZA

1
THE SCRUM

Those called to lead an exceptional life and ignore their vocation are hypnotised into a state of need and fall blindly into the daily scrum of the filthy normal. We are all exceptional.

2

THINNING

When a great sadness rises to the top, it invades the space where the skin is thin.

Sclerotic made sheer and the anger of others is nihilistic.

When the threat of death rings an alarm bell the skin morphs and thins out, trying to contain the emotions growing inside.

Exposing those we love to baleful fear, and so we walk. Solitude and the fight against the fear breaking down the door becomes the focus.

The battle begins.

3

ILLNESS

The threat of hurting those we love growls like a gnarled dragon ready to grind bones with mordant teeth. We did not mean to bring the dragon home. We try and fend it off with a sword, with positivity that glows in the hand. But arms can become so tired from swinging. The gravity of it is as old as time.

4
BIRTH

Flailing arms and cries, the rude awakening begins in a flat and heavy world where every pore is open to a million vibrations absorbing the bedlam. A radio active world where frequency hits neuron and neuron strikes the lines of the soul. Hold them close, they need it.

5

KINGDOM

Fear cannot break down the door when one does not exist.

A castle has no door, only a drawbridge and when the faithful hold the drawbridge firm, all that can be seen is a candle glowing within.

The dragon may still exist but is banished.

The halls are instead filled with love and laughter, drowning out the great sadness.

6
WE

You're going to be okay; we are all going to be okay.

7

ELECTRIC DANGER

The world is a busy place full of neurotic energy. Telluric currents charged with electric danger. People's hands catch on fire, they are thirsty for optimism in a barren place. A drought desires the rain like a lover.

Burning hands and parched hearts not ready for the storm.

8

SPACE IN BETWEEN

The passage of time between near-death and discovery is an eon and a second. A compounded moment of fear and stunning clarity that has every signal of the soul light up like a beacon.

9

THE TENDER WILD

The parent plays a lullaby sweet enough to nurture and be tender so not to strip away the wildness within. But when boundaries are placed lovingly firm to thrash against, the fences of consequence are understood.

10

NEED

You are the humanity by which I am supposed to learn my way. You have walked the path, burned the forests. Surely you hold the knowledge, surely you have discovered a way forward. Might you teach me or reduce my pain? Heal my trauma? The trauma is a lesson, not a prison. For the victim to become the warrior, don't they need a compassionate witness?

I THOUGHT YOU HAD MORE. I WAS BORN WITH A PROMISE YOU HAD MORE. More time, more love and calm. More peace and patience.

I WANT. WHY WAS I BORN WITH THIS PROMISE INSIDE ME? THIS EXPECTATION?

An unkind master, an empty box on a day of gifts. Needs.

AS I GROW, THE UNDERSTANDING UNFURLS LIKE A RIPPED RIBBON.

This is the way of things. So I shall snap these twigs between my thighs and start a fire because you have taught me well, and these things shall pass. My pain is mine alone, and it is the stretching of a soul. This is the more. I hid from it. Pushed away. But to transform it, one must walk through it and release it.

I SHALL LOVE YOU, BATHE YOUR FEET AND KNOW YOU AS BEST I CAN.

The box was never empty, and it was never a box at all; it was a message that said, I am so tired, my child. The needs are no longer and all that is left is love.

11

PROTECTION

We grow vines to protect our hearts, they can grow into the illusion of forests, dense and rich. God will always find you. It's your company God wants. You are loved. We are never hidden.

12

SERENDIPITY

I nfuse your gifts with love and care, for those receiving them are unwrapping pieces of you, your thoughts and joy. Serendipity is the greatest gift of them all.

13

SEEK

Violence and confusion are not easy to exist in. It is not a state the body copes with. The fraction of hope we witness in violent moments is a mere glitter shaving from a block of quartz the size of a mountain. Find the glitter, seek out the joy hiding beneath the pain and ask for help, you will find hope. You will climb the mountain.

14

ENTANGLEMENT

You can't rely anymore on the wisdom of the world, because now you have felt beyond it, behind it. An egg cannot go back into the embryo once cracked. You are untangled from the clatter. You have water to carry through the narrow gate. Feel the droplets of grace upon your soul.

15

BEYOND THE REALMS OF WORDS

Our ability to comprehend, evaluate and argue is reliant on the human brain. Yet, as impressively complex and productive as it is, the human brain has limitations. Perception and defence will always be the mechanics by which we act until we know a higher truth beyond the realms of thoughts.

16

THE SECRET

She woke from a sleep she did not have. She arrived back from a place she had no directions for. Everything felt different now. What once felt rich and beautiful was flat and sepia, and she was back inside the cave. They were trapped by what they thought it should be like and the extractions of their ideas. Some believed another world existed somewhere, and some were fatalistic. Now she knows.

17

DISCOVERY

We seek knowledge, yet when we find it, it cannot be unseen. We are forced out into the wilderness, leaving paradise behind. There can be dark times. Moments when the shades of humanity creep in, nuances of gross and heavy shadow behaviour are revealed. Do not be distracted by such things. The opportunity for growth has arrived. Find the quiet within, and clarity will prevail.

18

THE DEEP SADNESS

It can take many moons for the deep sadness to shift. In those times call for help, seek the greater outside of this skin and bone, and God will be felt. Enough to help you sleep and be soothed into calm again. A higher power calls you into calm and the promise of a delight greater than you can realise.

19

MOMENT

A tangible moment is all it takes to feel God's grace fall on your soul.

20
THE INVITATION

Please don't outsource your love and transcendence. I have waited so long.

21

FIREFLIES

Trying to catch reason is like catching a swarm of fireflies, to try and prove them to be electric. Blinking in and out of the line of sight, they venture far from the brink of think. Take a breath, do not ruminate, find the centre inside yourself and understanding will fall into your mind and heart and you will be glad because you will know the truth of things.

22

CUPS

If you stick with those reasons created by the fears and control of mankind you are trying to make a porcelain cup with mud.

23

SELF LOCKING CAGE

The moment I saw your lie
    was the instant I found me
        wanting, needing, chasing, wrapping my torn-worn blanket
    around my heart for comfort
    now I stand naked, strong, grounded, graceful, choosing
    free from my self-locking cage
    the pain is soothed by faith
    held firmly in place.
    I have arrived.

Vignettes of The Possibly Dying

24

FRIEND

We have lost some along the way, some by chance. Perhaps you left them in the street, left them at the market, they feel lost.

If they have left your life but not your heart, have they really left?

The unforgiven and the unfriended become stones in your pockets. Perhaps you wish they were not so. Perhaps you don't care a bit.

25

STONES IN OUR POCKETS

We wish our dance ends with tired happy feet, not ones broken and bruised. The stoush of life wears us down and we become tired of wanting. Shall we trap those who sit in our heart or wish them leave with love? For a handful of stones is all that is needed to make a pyre of regret. If we are to fly we cannot have stones in our pockets.

26

CURIOUS

Be curious about forgiveness, surrender to releasing those who hold you. Because you hold them also.

27

MORE

A brain can only conceive of the forms and dimensions it projects. So much is hidden. Your brain is wonderful but it is not everything.

28

THRUM OF NEED

We hear what we want to hear, even when our Inner self might be screaming at the top of her lungs, trapped in a cage we did not mean to make for her. We are like a locksmith who forgot where the key is hidden and she becomes a whisper. All we hear is the thrum of our need, drowning out choices until they are scrambled or eliminated altogether. Entanglement feels like knots in our hearts. Listen child. Those knots don't need to exist.

29

THE PROMISE

ith each sun rise we are promised that as long as we search for light we will find it.

30

DARK SEEDS CANNOT GROW

We can be like a child in calm innocent contemplation. Inspired but not jaded. The truth can light the corners of where lies hide. Dark seeds cannot grow in the bright illumination of which you are a part. My protection is yours , you are never alone.

31

DARK DANDELIONS

Lies grow into dark dandelions and when the wind blows a certain way and the conditions are met the seeds release and blow onto all those around them. Planting into the hearts and minds of others. A contagion, a pollen that threatens hardship. Those are the seedlings of chaos, of conflict, fuel for the self righteous.

32

THE BINDING

We will want the love and presence of the parent who denies us until the day we die. But we must understand the trauma from small children binds the adult and seeks pain to create itself again and again. See the trauma in the parent, explore understanding the components of it and your own healing can begin.

33

NOTE TO SELF

Remove the mask and release the thoughts of self; rattling around amongst the frumble. Put down the measuring stick that has left your back bruised and bloody. Stroke your skin and wriggle your toes. You are alive, you are wonder in motion.

34

SENTRY

The leaf you see on the surface is only the tip of a deep rooted tree that believes it is a mere piece of foliage. Until someone sings to it, reminding it of its sacred duty. It then becomes a sentry, and a teller of stories.

35

THE VOICE

We make words and sounds with twirls and twists of the tongue through a voice box to produce understanding between us. A sound is made and posted; acoustic waves like a letter with wings across space to a passageway. Bouncing along bones and forest floors its frequency delivers it to the tuning place, where it is unfolded gently and organised into the next jour- ney; perception. But what of the place it travels to? Is it a hostile place where soldiers have erected fortresses and only understand commands? Perhaps it is a field of trodden sunflowers breaking their backs to see the sun, taking the letter and holding it for life.

There is a place where words are not needed and sounds are the harmonies projecting kindness and heart. The journey is so treach- erous and compromising, unknown and dangerous. The truth might be seen and understood. This place where grass is as green as polished emeralds and sand could tell the tales of a millennia in a touch.

But for now, understand that all we see and hear are illusions and echoes. Listen to your inner voice, seek God. Seek love.

36

SELF

Will you love me if I am changed? If I am altered from the original person you fell in comfort with? If you were attracted to my freedom, will you be attracted to my scars?

If you were in love with my gentle nature, will you be in love with the fierce woman I have become? Or will you change? Will the young me and the old me stretch too far apart and grow unrecognisable or shall we rejoice in the newness of our transformations? Will my eyes go from green to blue and our conversations run dry? Will I look at you with compassion and hold you close when you need it most?

Your journey into being, transcending the heaviness of the world means you must explore how to love the being beneath your skin, one the eyes cannot see. The divine being made in an image and given the opportunity to grow in harsh conditions of the fleshy vessel.

37

CONSCIOUSNESS

A divine code is denied, the edge of chaos is used and gathered. The primordial sludge is unimportant and yet it knows all and believes in nothing. Do we friction against the universe? Are we random fluctuations, skin, tissue and bone alone or will the soul surpass the sinew without explanation? Birds fly together, ants build together and we are not random. We never were.

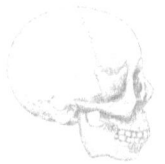

38

THE TEACHER

What good is a teacher who whispers the words to the child writing their own story?

39

SIGNALS

Hidden thoughts and agendas are secret signals. Find clues for their motivation, but do not make them yours.

40

THE ETHER

You cannot touch the ether without bringing the sand back on your feet.

41

NOT ALONE

You are not alone; you are never alone.

42

WHAT IF?

What if your crisis breaks the bonds of your captured life? What if it becomes the catalyst to change the world with one footprint? Wouldn't this be interesting?

43

OSCILLATION

What riddle irritates the human mind so much that requires us to feel satiated and complete when we understand the door, what is behind it and how it closes? The mechanisms evade us and we frown, or we discover and we smile. Closure and acknowledgement oscillate with a whirl and a wrinkle in our contemplative mind. The search for meaning begins with truth, find the truth and hold it dear even if it scorches your hands.

44

SLY

When thoughts are undisciplined and unruly, they become sly playmates.

45

SOUL IN ANIMATION

Tandem incarnations from a star adrift on a notion of forever, stretching far to the reaches of the sky's edge. This is not the way of things; we are deliberate, and we are in action, we are here, we are now. Life is a soul in animation, not a floating essence.

46

PLATFORMS

Often people who are revered have found themselves there through the adoration of unempowered people seeking cures for the heart instead of looking within and to God. Be careful who you place yourself below.

47

FEAR OF DEATH

The fear of death is born from the fear of the separation of the physical. As a species it runs deep within us, fears are perceptions, they are not facts.

48

CONSEQUENCES

Consequence is a word we hold in our hand like a strange seed. Which garden shall we plant that in? The one that faces the north and screams of victim or the one that whispers growth? The best garden may be daunting for those that have walked the old paths and remember their twists and turns. Those will be cleared and newness can be glimpsed through the bracken and weeds, overgrowing the walls.

49

NOW

Tomorrow sits on the threads of the sunset, elusive and strange. Your life is now, the next minute might be new if you let it.

50

THE CHILD

Blame is the stamping foot of an angry child, anger is the fear of the lonely child and laughter is the child finding their way home.

51

LOVE TONIC

Hope, faith and discernment helps defend the body against disease and encourages repair of cellular structures. A peaceful and calm body is a restored one. A body that can experience real love, connection and bonding to soul, each other and to God. This is the most important thing of all.

52

NEWNESS

They will visit and wonder at the shape of you now, your newness, your battle clothes and the fire that now burns brightly all around you. They will learn to know you. It is just going to take some time.

53

MAKE STILL THE CHAOS

The chaos around us and within us stimulate our senses, our means for interpretation. There is a vastness to the sensory information we absorb. We are identifying with our suppressions, and the murky waters deep within begin to gurgle. When we are still and we self-monitor, we can become unentangled. We can then explore and observe the subliminal; freedom waits.

54

OPPORTUNITY

They were never meant to suffer, and yet here they are, given the opportunity to remember joy.

55

MONSTERS

The shadows of humans can be monstrous and asphyxiating, manipulating nature like dictators. Between the ears is the enemy, bending the will and changing the truth.

56

SLENDER THE NIGHT

This night may feel slender, punctuated by thoughts and restlessness. Cells repair and hearts build in this vast universe we call a being. Tiny explosions, buildings and battles are raging on in a ballet of fusions without conscious awareness, all of its own accord. The automation is readjusting, rebuilding, propagating a life force. Get some sleep. You need it.

57

EVAPORATE

Hope hits hard and we try and shield away from it, like torrential rain that threatens to flood and retreat like a teasing enemy. Because sometimes hope feels like an impossible demand. But letting the rain hit your face offering your skin to its touch, makes the fear evaporate like water on a hot road.

58

THE BELONGING

I am free. I feel no pain, I can feel love, so big my chest feels like it will explode into a star dust and hearts, love, tears, expansion and ecstasy. Tiny bells, tinker gently. Electrified, sharp, laughter, the beaming realisation of no restraint. The belonging returns.

59

LIFE

This is not a test.
    This is not a punishment This is a university with icebergs, trees and bad breath. This is possibility.
When do the drummers drum?
When they feel the rhythm call.
Each beat pulls at their heart and feels movement. It is time.

60

SHE

The women have strength that is not to be feared. Trust the shaking breast and belly, the fullness screaming to be heard, so be seen and felt and to love. The violinist must play the violin, as the woman must live in a world where she can love. They will love you endlessly and thoroughly if you let them, it is time to let show her all your hidden places. She is tougher than muscle, braver than wind and as mighty as the sun after a storm. Do not believe the lies. Believe in the version of you that craves to be whole.

61

BUTTONS

Time is not a commodity. It is the most precious and delicate aspect of our existence. Without it, we are nothing but buttons clinking together in a giant's pocket and telling each other we end now.

62

NOBLE DANGER

What if their intentions are wonderful? This does not matter. If you are not standing in your soul filled power when you make a decision then it is not for you. Other people's intentions can be a subconscious need to fuel desire, to be loved, to be respected, to be needed, to seek control, to seek importance. A noble idea can be sweet to the ears, but it may well be a self-based agenda none-the-less.

63

BEAUTIFUL HEARTS

The surrendered and non-agendered heart is beautiful.

64

SUPERNATURAL MARKET

If we become consumed with the distractions of the world, we miss the magnificence of what we can experience now. There is no supernatural market from which to purchase God.

65

PARADOX

Connection with each other, while we walk our own path, is as important as our state of being. Our relationships with each other are the experience through which we develop our course. The two cannot be separated but must be parallel and singular. The paradox is the balance of the two.

66

ARE YOU READY?

There is only now. Do you have those shoes on your feet and a tune in your pocket? Are you ready for the tiniest step and butterfly of an idea to lead into a mighty treasure hunt filled with rewards that lift you up out of the fen and into the truth of everything you are here to do?

67

STONES THROWN

If your actions are from a mind that tries consciously or subconsciously to interrupt the fabric of another or break the road they walk to rubble-take caution. Intentions with or without remain stones thrown.

68

UNSEEN HANDS

Fallen bridges can be rebuilt, each shattered rock joined with another, the mortar held fast by an unseen hand. Reaching out and connecting us to a land we never even thought of. Beyond the edges of our planning or control.

69

BREACH

Mass amnesia is live-streamed across the oceans and lands as we climb and stomp over an all too tolerant earth we were gifted. We have forgotten we are a species with instincts, love, skilful intelligence and wisdom at our core. The faculty of natural connection is getting lost in translation. The world is dominated by the species of human, the physicality of it that en masse believes it has all of the answers.

Conceptualisation has limitations and is a deceptive barrier. You must reach beyond the ego and also listen within for guidance.

70

SURRENDER

Surrender is not the making of a puppet begging the master for movement. Surrender is not giving up; it is powerful, potent and energising, loving and not for the faint of heart. As we move from control to release; conflict arises, as awareness and knowledge cannot exist without the unravelling of long-held beliefs. Remembering the path you were on and must walk again, disconnecting from the hypnosis of your nest is no easy thing to do. But you can. When you do, the brilliance will be blinding.

71

DESTINY UNCHALLENGED

Space matter, minerals and infinite energy went into this existence, do not waste it while it lasts in this experience. The clock ticks, the circadian rhythm, thump, thump, thump. If your path is to raise incredible future generations or stop a child from being hit by a car on a warm summer day-so be it. If your path is to cure the diseases caused by generations of genetic accumulation-so be it. If your path is to travel the world and advocate for those without freedom that need their human rights returned to them, for this was always meant to be, so be it. But will it be so? If you choose it.

72

SLAVES TO THE BIGGER

Slaves to the bigger we are not. We are not contained, we imagine we are. Another person's power is paltry compared to the effusion of life. You cannot use a ruler to measure life any more that you can harness a star with a vine. You are part of an intricate ever evolving creation more amazing than you could ever imagine.

73

UNBRINGING

The feelings are so big in the battlefield of children, trying to find their voice. Playing out the scripts of their upbringing and unbringing while they find music to play.

74

WITNESS

No longer owned by the flesh of fear, you are to dance, and it will be glorious for the worlds more than these grant your witness to the extraordinary. You can understand and feel the warmth from the sun of God's grace. This is your Invictus.

75

GOLDEN

No sword is made golden without flame and hammer.

76

CHILD RESTORED

Even when you were small you knew this place was like broken glass and filled with shadowy hidden things. Your panic subsided when you started to shut down, but now, now you know. It was all real. It is time to release those acts and shadows that do not belong to you. They never did. It is time to step into the light. You will be restored, by surrender and surrender alone.

77

A PRAYER TO SELF

I HAVE TREATED YOU LIKE A SLAVE WITH BLOODIED FEET AND A WEARY heart, forcing you to trod through the sharp bracken and steely rocks. I ignored your pleas. I pretended I could not hear your shaking voice. Until you stopped and would no longer move. I'm so sorry. I didn't mean to ignore you. I forgive us. You don't believe me anymore. I have made so many promises, mundane denials. Your joy and your balance, your prosperity and love will be my quest. This is my promise.

78
FREE

You are no longer a prisoner. You are loved.

79

POST HASTE

The message is for the person sitting in a lab somewhere, drinking coffee to stay awake, grappling with the missing code just on the edge of their brain, they are within a moment's reach of that discovery, one that could save thousands of lives, please hurry. For the Mother thinking of taking a second shift so her daughter can do studies that will help discover a gene to save humanity, please hurry and thanks.

To the young man who thinks of the treasure in his bones as he reads a story, hear my call. The butterfly that landed on your shoulder, beckoning you to act is more significant than you know. Please do not lose sight, my friend opening this message because people have discovered what it is to be fearless, they have found faith as an act of friendship, and they want to stay and experience more. Something is coming.

POST HASTE.

KB ELIZA

80

LITTLE MOUSE

There was a little mouse, who was a kind and happy mouse, always looking after the other mice. One day her leg broke. Then she had three legs instead of four. She was sick for a very long time and lived in a cold little hole in a wall with bugs. The doctor mouse told her she would never recover. Never is a very big word for a small mouse. Many of the other mice were scared to come near her, for they were worried they might get sick too, but most of all they didn't want to feel her sadness. The little mouse became lonely. This made her very glum.

One night the little mouse looked out from her hole and saw hope hanging from the sky like a star. She put her little paws up and held the image of it in her heart and part of her believed she captured some. The next day she woke up and decided not to give up. She believed goodness was coming her way. She had the days when she cried, and felt her feelings. Then the day arrived when her heart filled to the brim with sunshine, like a basket of peaches and fond thoughts of tomorrow. It was like a rainbow.

. . .

Then one day, her miracle arrived. Her sickness faded. Her pale fur became brown again. She felt glorious and so very grateful. For a miracle is scarce and a super special thing indeed. She said her prayers and gave thanks, and the most wonderful things began to

happen. She found a new hole to live in with no bugs, it was cosy and warm.

She was faster than ever on her three legs and with good use of her tail, she was quicker than the other mice. Watch her go! The other mice would exclaim as she flew by like lightning. This prosperity was a welcome gift.

Then the strangest thing happened. One day those she held dear no longer came out of their holes. A great hunger overcame them. Hiding away they ate and ate, they ate their feet, their little mouse tails and their memories until they all became too big and got stuck.

Aghast the little mouse missed them, and she begged them to come outside. She tried to sing to them, she left food outside for them to nibble on, but the only thing they would cry out was -Where's Mine?

They were happy for the little mouse, but they were hungry too, miracles are the very best of feasts and how their tummies rumbled. For no one resents a miracle, but everyone starves for one also.

. . .

Vignettes of The Possibly Dying

The little mouse became lonely again, and no longer wanted to be separate. So she tucked herself into her petite mouse house, and scratched and nibbled away at the miracle until it was all worn and nobody noticed it anymore. In between bites, she whispered to the other mice between the walls. They talked about mouse things, nothing at all special. She was so busy doing this, bugs snuck into her house and started making a mess.

She forgot about her gift.
She no longer had a calamity.
She no longer had prosperity.
She wanted to feel safe.
She might have stayed there forever. But something niggled at her little mouse heart. It wasn't a shout, because the best niggles always start out quiet. The niggle told her that staying there and forgetting her miracle was very wrong.

SO SHE DID WHAT ALL BRAVE LITTLE MICE DO, SHE PACKED UP, PUT SOME hope in her pocket and set out for an adventure. Because adventures aren't always easy, but they always show their worth it in the end.

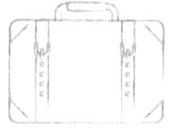

81

THE LIE

You believe it is death you want, but it is escape. You believe in the illusions and the shadows on the walls, and in the darkness a great sickness grows within. Your actions will breathe life into a deeper sadness for those who need you. They will be scarred. You will change the course of their lives forever, like a dam in a river meant to flow. The lie will tell you otherwise but I tell you the truth. It is time to live. This too shall pass.

82

CALL MY NAME

Call my name. Surrender your pride and give your self over. One step at a time. It's going to be okay.

83
YES

You are beginning.

84

THREADS

We wear layers like the stories we are told. We have worn them so long the fibres are etched into our skin. We keep this hidden skin, but we must be careful. The loose threads that no longer serve us will bind us. Threads need trimming, this is what our ancestors want for us, and it only comes from the stillness. That worldly place makes our senses run like a bear with his paws on fire, and we do not know it. We smell the smoke but do not know what it is. So you must remember to put your paws in the water. Be still and knowledge will arrive like a long lost friend.

Vignettes of The Possibly Dying

85

MIRTH

You believe you have all the answers, but you are standing in your ruptured ideas. This is an impossible way to remember your path and meaning. You must know truth. For whilst we grow through hardship, it need not be desolate and barren, there is mirth to experience. There will be peace.

86

WASH AWAY

A yoke, a harness dictating the direction of the field to be ploughed. A story in a play you do not want to act in. Years of playing in the game created by others, a game of personality and ego projecting shadows on a wall. Wash away, wash away now and into a future bright, uncommon and in alignment with your soul.

87

CHOICES

It is your decision and yours alone. Because this is your life.

88

ANCHOR

An anchor in a chaotic world can be hard to find. So be the anchor. Breathe deeply, put your heels to the ground or palms to the floor. Say out loud I am here. I am safe. I am surrounded by the protection of God's mighty hand.

89

BUTTERFLY

Gone in a breath, in a look, in a minute. One moment they were butterflies and the next the powder fell from their wings, leaving them faded and dying. No longer a vessel of inspiration for the mammoth souls anchored to this flat, dense world.

They reel from the shock when it happens, flittering from flower to flower, from nectar to bud, ear to ear. The unfairness of it all, they whispered to each other. How? Why? This was not what she wanted for them surely? To be ignored, or discarded or changed?

One person feels the butterfly on their shoulder and marvels at the notion of a new ingredient, but remembers to check the news and the butterfly falls. Others pull the wings from their small bodies cutting their journey short with arguments. Those that believed in their own wisdom told stories about a maker of butterflies who was punishing and others said there was nothing at all but space and butterflies were mere insects.

The sound of wings snapping and powder falling, was the crushing of inspiration, sending an echo across the universe of ideas unfulfilled.

THE BUTTERFLIES KNEW THESE BEINGS HELD LIVES DESIGNED TO BE FULL and to learn and experience this place. But they cannot and do not live here forever. They must return from where they came to share the stories of their travels. It was a long journey and the ideas for the awe didn't come from inside their heads.

90

CONTROL

Control is ceased render-less when we walk forward with love.

91

OLD STORY NEW BEGINNING

The codex is old, but so is the story. Our story doesn't end, it begins.

92

MY CHILD

All I want is for you is to tread with bravery and discernment; because they are the best companions for a successful adventure. That path you walk is full of holes. I stand breathless watching you walk it, knowing I must not steal your steps or give you too many clues to the way. I must not piggyback you or carry you over the rocks. Because down the way, there will be boulders, so rocks must be navigated first. That old enemy fear, its ironic tendrils may throttle your heart and loss must not be my legacy for you! It is a weighted basket of foul panic and baked loneliness you are forced to carry, because you cannot get letters from heaven. You may hate me and see me as the wolf who stole your happiness.

I do not want to make you feel like when you were small in a market and you could not find me, that panicked moment when who you thought you were following was not me at all, not yours. All alone. For isn't this the cruelest trick? I do not want to damage you, I do not want to spoil you, I do not want to leave you, all I want to do is help you be all you were meant to be in the way you need me to help you. I am here. I have always been here.

93

CONJURER

I will build you an internal castle, and raise you up to its towers so you may look out upon the lands and let your dreams float wildly like a conjurer of a storm.

94

THE GREAT SICKNESS

The tribe sat around the crackling fire, baffled and withered. The palaver lasted for months. Tears and anger, frustration and the great sadness swept through their lands.

A nefarious disease had befallen them, a dreadful thing growing inside their bodies, multiplying and hacking. Why did this disease continue to grow in them? Stealing their mothers, fathers and children?

The medicine people of the tribe tried and studied, as the butterflies fluttered against the windows. They toiled and travelled looking for answers, discovering new remedies, mixtures and concoctions that could help battle the disease. Yet the condition eluded them.

The tribe started to believe the doctors were making the medicine to make money. Some shouted to the Gods - Why do you punish us so? Other stood on boxes and yelled at their tribe-We are wrong, and we must suffer, this is why there is a disease, we are being punished!

The mystics in the tribe cried out as they ruffle their feathers-

These are debts we owe the stars that we must pay regardless of the price. This is not real, if you wish this to be gone it will be so, if you place this magical seed under your tongue, it will be gone. But this was wishing of hopeful hearts.

Only listening carefully to the sound of the sickened body and listening closely, for inside each tribes-person was a wondrous universe full of messages waiting to be discovered. The tribespeople did not believe they chose the sickness, it was not their doing.

But in truth, the tribe and the doctors and the mystics did not understand. The condition of being human, bodies morphing in ways to adapt, and all glitches are chaos in motion. Inertia shattered. Disease is not the making of a wizard in a cloudy dream. Disease is the accumulation of genetics, of decisions and of freewill and ancestral choices manifesting into form and creation. God does not create disease, God whispers answers into the hearts of medicine people trying to ease pain.

The messages were not coming through, the story of free will. The alterations growing from the choices of every ancestral line formed the puzzle pieces they hold in their bodies.

They were the great inventor species holding dominion and choice. They decayed and devolved. This was growth in all its spectrum in light and shade; emergence. The medicine people and the tribespeople that still held fierceness in their hearts and hope in their feet made a plan. There was a song heard in the whispers of the wind, and they listened.

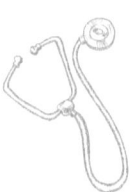

95

DIVINE BODY

The energy you create with your body is a divine mechanism. Capable of feats you have yet to discover. How might you express it?

96

BENEATH HER SKIN

She looked at her skin and asked to be shown. Show me. Show me us. The pearly luminous light beneath revealed a divine beauty the world had projected lies upon. She saw the truth of woman and finally understood. It was so big and threatening to the ego, a power wanting to be so important it sought to steal and break her into pieces. The time for lies is over.

97

BROKEN DOLLS

Every doll that had arms broken off and faces painted were made new again and the dark hearts that sort to discard them were put away on a shelf. She stood in radiant glory and he stood in grace and wisdom and wonder. They delighted in their acceptance and beauty. They all stood on the sand and watched the sun rise without label, without judgement nor word. For such truth and magnificence could not have a sound attributed to it. It stretched beyond any such thing.

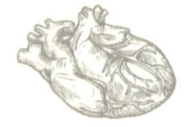

98

TOKENS

e are like bower birds finding tokens as replacements for that which we lack within.

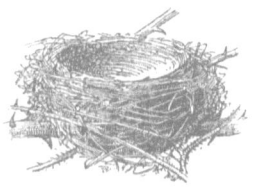

99

SHOW ME

Do not pick a flower for me, show me your heart. This will last forever.

100

YOU ARE NOT YOU ARE

You are not a mark upon the earth, a stain reeking of inimical havoc. You are a divine being who may be tricked into slavery and charmed into the marketplace. This false world will fall away when you search God out.

101

DELICATE FINGERPRINTS

When we are in service to another in a way that seeks to empower them, they might find their own truth. Their path is a delicate fingerprint you cannot draw with a pencil.

102

HOME

We are born, we live, we die? No.
We are created in this form and we learn and return home. Life from emergence to transformation is a quest. There is a place where you can touch the grass, be in the grass, shapes within shapes and radiating colours unimaginable that will have you laughing and crying with the joy of recognition.

103

THE CROSS

They know not what they do, but they are starting to understand.

104

SIP THY TEA

A discerning heart cannot deny the truth. The warm hearth and soothing tea steeps our senses, a tonic for the broken to stay still. You cannot stay there forever. The time is coming soon. You will be ready.

105

FOR I AM LOVED

Fill my heart with your grace, so my heart's deep ache might lessen. Reduced enough to not lose the understanding, but to be able to withstand the present as it passes. The sun will rise and I will know a time greater than this and more beautiful than I have ever known. For I am loved by an unseen hand and held by unseen arms.

106

IDEA LIFE HACK

Rest, sitting beneath stars, patting a dog and being in commune together is the way we can use our time effectively. It is in the quiet and the energy of nature that the essential ideas arrive.

107

OBSERVATIONS

When the hardship is part of our journey we will feel the small synchronisations, the little acts of kindness from others, or the sparrow that lands near our hand. A higher power is always watching and all things are working together to restore you and pull you out of the mire into the light. If you cannot see these signs, get out as soon as you can and get to a place of light and love. You are not in the right place. Find shelter from the storm in any way you can.

108

INERTIA

The inertia of our lives screams for dissidence and change whilst hiding in the corner begging to be found, begging to be touched. The paradox is painful and we can rise above it. Come out from the corner, it's going to be okay.

109

NEW WORLD WITHIN

What does a new world look like? What will it be? Whatever we want it to be. But first there must be truth and self-realisation.

110

COMMODITY

They build these structures and trinkets, fabrics and gadgets, these skin and tissue imitations to view and create beauty around us. Cheap replicas of what was already made for us. Beauty shines back to you every day in the tree branch and trunk with its knotted history and deep resounding formation. The river water running by offering its reflection of everything around us. A beautifully made river.

Why must the water reflect? It is its nature to do so you see. For when the water no longer reflects the sky and the trees, the mirror is left filthy by unappreciative hands, moving it from house to house, leaving coffee stains on it. We borrow these words from them. For we know not 'house', only home.

Beneath the surface, the universe that resides inside is crushed and degraded with the aftermath of grubby hands. For water is now a commodity, its barriers, its ability all traded for these boney shiny carbon copies. As they try and forget from where they came and try to become more, more more. Yet around them, the magnificent home around them cries out less, less, less.

They have broken all the archways, torn down the walls, smashed the mirrors, and discarded their wrappings.

The beauty tries to shine through to remind them they are the caretakers of all of this. It was designed to provide sustenance, life, peace and inspiration.

Their rank wrecking and destruction must be the work of a species trying to manifest its own demise from hatred.

SADLY, THE VIOLENCE AGAINST EACH OTHER AND OF THESE LANDS IS AN action that comes from heaviness and damaged minds. This is not of the light and has nothing to do with their source. This is a tragic consequence of humanity adjusting with adapted perceptions and filters, producing the big lie. It is time for truth.

111

I SEE YOU

Only when the broken have left with their baubles and bangles, their suits with words and parking lots, we will sit beneath the trees that give us air, we will touch our foreheads to the tree's skin and say thank you. Thank you for being so brave.

112

EGO

They are like actors in a darkened hall, kinematic inventors, emotional projectiles smashing into the world. Ignorant of the dynamics at play in the ancient theatre. Its dim curtain raised and lowered by unobservable entities. Chaos and harmony colliding. The unbalanced force of many small actions has tipped resistance and accelerate at lightning speed to consciousness, or will they take their final bow?

113

HUNGER

This is the truest quest my friends, to remember our truth. The greatest poverty is the hunger for love under the misguidance of emotional violence.

114

THE SWORD

I cut away the darkness around me with an illuminated sword of silver. Thorny branches are slashed and severed. I take them and burn them with all the flames of love I can find and as the smoke rises into healing- I give thanks. Claim back all that has been taken from you. You can find the holes left by the actions of others and tend to your wounds. You can take back your power and hold your grace.

115

GOD

When you look to each direction, look for me. In the rising and lowering sun we move in its light set in motion by hands larger than you can imagine. The frequency made by the beat of a bee's wings and the polarity between two grains of sand are delights for you to witness and remember from where you came and where it is you go again once your work is done.

116

JOURNEY ON

Death is not a punishment. As each person makes their journey home they begin a pilgrimage and action deeds small and large, so powerful they will ripple across what we call dimensions into eternity. It is painful and powerful beyond our understanding. But you must know you do not end. You begin. You go on to a place realer than our world, bigger, and more beautiful than you can possibly conceive. It is beyond our limited perspective, beyond our time and measurement. You must know this and take peace from it. Seeking out harmony is the tonic to balance the learning. What awaits is worth the journey.

117

FREE WILL

Every one of us has free-will to such intricate extremes our neurons respond on a quantum level. Decisions and choices are not whimsy. They are the roads we choose our adventures. Like threads in a blanket. Which is why you must never pull or the threads on another person's blanket.

118

MURDEROUS GEM

nowledge is the next coveted jewel. People will mock it, strangle it into submission and even kill for it.

119

ESCAPE TO THE NOW

Some try very hard in this world to connect to a realm with a wanting, a desire to be home again. To be not in this world. To get there, to be knowledgable here. But here is the space in which we dwell. Here is where we are for a time. Home is from where we came and will return. But we are here and now. We have eternity for there. If you watch closely you will see the divine under the skin, in the branch of a tree, in the shine of a babies eye. You will see it leave also and know what it is to glimpse divinity and the horror of its absence. You are safe and there is joy lying just beneath the surface, not in a far away place but here in your heart with your feet on the ground.

120

MATCHES

Delving into the egoic layer of knowledge and holding external power over others is a dangerous journey. People yearn to own a sense of importance, but these are the tricks of a non-precise language. Wrangling with stories we do not know in an attempt to make sense of the world and our place in it. But we must not try and create facts. This is like flicking a small stone into machinery so complex, ancient and sacred we can do damage to another person's journey.

Every person is a creation of divinity and can open their hearts to God. It is a promise as old as creation. Manfesting this into form dilutes the calm and opportunity for self-realisation.

WE ARE LIKE CHILDREN PLAYING WITH MATCHES IN A DRY FOREST, we know nothing about. It is time to be humble, to listen, to know and learn and to help each other in no one's name but Gods.

Vignettes of The Possibly Dying

121

COMPANION, WHEREFORE ART THOU?

The time for power over each other is over. Betrayal runs deep. We project our fear of loneliness on another, looking for lost treasure in them when it's God we really seek. Humans are not meant to be idols we worship. We are friends and kin. But first we must be our own companions.

122

UNIVERSAL ETHER

The joy we have in playing with our ideas, our intuitions and dreams are memories of home plucked from a universal ether and expressed in art and form. Inspiring and reminding us to strive and glimpse the purpose of our time here creating.

123

FRIEND IN THE DARKNESS

It is not easy. This life is absolutely and entirely, not comfortable. It is a place for us to learn, and when we have the grace of our creator in our lives as an active tour guide, it is better. God is a complete mystery, and yet the necessary friend we need to get to the other side with love and light in our hearts. It doesn't have to be a dark and lonely path. We were never meant to suffer, and yet here we are, given the opportunity to remember love, to work diligently through.

124

QUESTS

Decisions are not made by stethoscopes, heroes are made but quests are another matter entirely.

125

BODIES

Getting as close to our natural state in these bodies as we can is necessary to provide sustenance so we can experience the existential miracle of life here and now. God is everywhere. In the shape of a cloud, the rings of a tree, the curl of a shell, every formula, quark and photon. If we become consumed with the distractions of the world, we miss the magnificence.

126

DISAGREEMENT WITHIN

The well-balanced mind does not submit to carnage voluntarily by another hand. The inner confusion and turmoil in the decision to agree for the body to be damaged to continue living is not natural. Seek to heal, seek the truth. You are brave.

127

THE DIRT OF DAYS

May your fingernails be filled with the dirt of days and determination. The sense of a war is ending. You cannot rescue yourself. But you can be restored. You can reach out, ask for help. For you are mighty. You are strong. You are wanted.

128

THE SWELL

Droplets of understanding fall into the mind and marvel expands so much it feels as though the skin of your chest may rupture from the volume, fattened and swollen. Big, small, big small, the focus comes in and out and the euphoria threatens to burst like a balloon filled with water from a tap. This is the swell. This is what it is to know God.

129

ANGRY THIRST

We must show mercy to those sitting in anger for they're longing. One day they will know it, and it will be a refreshing drink on a hot day, parching an angry thirst.

130

WOMAN

She is curve, soft flesh and mighty soul. She is grace, she is love and fury in motion. Shoulder, breast, lips, earlobe, her hips and the creases from smiling. The belly that has been filled with life or experiences. The pink of her fingernail and the white puckering of skin - the markings of the warrior.

131

THE DOOR

If you have been presented with a lie, if someone has deceived you give thanks. Life just opened a door for you, a new opportunity just arrived in unexpected packaging.

132

THE FRIEND

Friendship is about sharing, not extracting.

133

CREATION IN MOTION

The joy in expression must never be underestimated or made to be folly. It is a quest we were made for. We are creation in motion.

134

WIFE

Talk to her. Hold her hand and become curious. She is not all known yet. She is a beautiful land waiting to be discovered, loved and explored and she is truly a stranger to you. It is in appreciation of the mystery that joy can be found and held close.

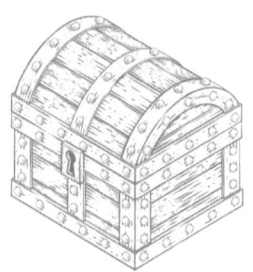

135

DAYS

Honour your days with acts of kindness to yourselves and others.

136

SHADOWS

When we want to control others to be victors in competition, game or fear -we steal away our opportunity to heal the dark parts of ourselves.

137

THIEF IN THE NIGHT

The expectations of others will steal your moments like a thief in the night. Guard your home well, know your heart and follow your truth. There is no other way. The price for not following truth is too big for you to pay in this life.

138

SEAMS

The other place is so close I could stretch my hand through the air, running my thumb along an invisible seam, curling back a curtain. The curling of a cone, the twist in a shell, the slip between feels like I am breath away from home.

139

INNOCENCE

The heart that can see another in simple actions is blessed with the best kind of vision.

140

MY BODY

I am sorry you were feeling so alone and confused. I am sorry your heart felt it needed rest and your strife felt never ending. I send you love and hold you close and envelope you in uncountable blessings so that you will heal and feel whole once more.

141

ESCAPING THE CAVE

She walks the dance between fear and light. The rock bed beneath steadies the way. The fear bubbles and breaks against the froth passing mightily away to another place. For the day goes and shadows no longer linger. The cave has opened and the light streams unhindered, and so it is.

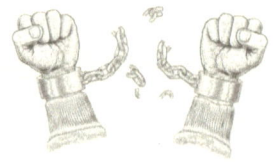

142

SEE THEM

Give someone a word of encouragement today. If you sense their goodness, tell them.

143

JESUS

He will pull you into the boat from the depths of the dark and drowning sea. He will dry you, give you clothing of finest threads. In return he will ask you to be the watch keeper in the lighthouse watching for your kin with waves lapping over their heads, and hearts starting to panic. This is the way of God.

144

INTOXICATION

Reach to me, yield to me. Take claim and power over this problem. Shake the intoxication from off your skin and be ready for the future is here and it is yours.

145

THE TECH SIRENS

Strangers and darklings that sparkle of false beauty on black mirrors are like fireflies luring us to the shadowy forest. Stretched and swollen flesh cannot hold the sun.

146

PLEASURE

God is not shame or denial of pleasure. But pleasure is not empty. Pleasure is the enthusiasm of the soul to seek out another in playfulness without traumatising. Empty touching is death of the soul by a million small cuts. The moment our mind or body reaches out to touch another the intention must be known and it cannot be hungry, consuming or greedy. We can traumatise ourselves and others under the pretence of simplicity when we are really fumbling with dynamite.

147

ATOMIC

The woman restored is a sun amongst tiny planets. She must claim back her power, grace will fill the holes that deceive her making her believe she has faded. She is atomic and will fill the hearts of eternity and the darkness will be no more. So it is.

148

CLOSE YOUR EARS

Death, abandonment and the displeasure of others are not the tunes you need heed.

149

DANCE

Dance to the songs of your grace, your inheritance is joy and it waits for you.

150

HIDING PLACES

Liberation can only come after the trauma has been stripped bare and there are no more hiding places.

151

THE MANIFESTATION

We are creation manifested into form. Self-actualised instruments of magnificence.

152

BORN AGAIN

Her chest feels empty, faint and eaten alive. Hands shake, and her blood sugar falls with the pieces of her heart.
    She feels she might die, but she is being born. Again, and again and again.

153

THE HORROR OF BEAUTIFUL TRUTH

They smash the world apart with swords, dark power filled eyes in hidden places. They cry at all they have broken. Desperate hands and tricksters discover the truth of their beauty within and weep at the carnage.

154

FAIRYTALES

Princes pretending to be Kings and Goddesses masquerading as tired Princesses tending to the kitchen. Where have the children gone?

155

DEATH OF EGO

Strangers stealing love away with swift hands in the dark until the lightning hits. The castle burns to the ground. The broken crawl into the sun, crowns are gone and the jesters are turned away. The kings or queens are gone. Love and wonder restored. Oh my, how they shine.

156

DO YOU WANT TO BE HEALED?

There is beauty in vulnerability; there is no reason to feel ashamed or lessened. Do you want to be healed?

157

SEDUCTION

The tempting and alluring siren song will call you into to the ocean. Cooling water on hot skin. Mystical movement, song and exotic colours. Soothing numbness.

Then your feet cannot touch the bottom. The sky turns dark, the clouds roll in.

The drowning begins.

158

LIGHT KILLED THE BEAST

Fear is a beast that becomes a whimper when faced with hope and faith. Once the light enters, it is consigned to oblivion or impelled to slumber on.

159

FORGIVENESS

When people lack respect for themselves they cannot find it for others. Disrespect is a nasty tonic to taste. You want to spit it out, repulsed and inflicted. To show respect to someone after you have sipped their poison is difficult. Yet grace can be found in the most unlikely of places and love can prevail.

160

THE JOURNEY

We are here for a time, we learn and we return.

161

TREASURE

A friend is no longer just someone you like to spend time with. A friend is a treasure, another soul on a journey that rides beside you for a time and may remind you of what it is to be loved and laughed with.

162

RISE

Rise up child. Show the world who you are. You were made in divine grace, the darkness can no sooner cover it then a towel might cover the sun.

163

REMOVE THE MASK

There is a chance for them all to be loved in a way their hearts calls, but they dance to the voice of the singer, laugh at the jester and eat their fill from the cook until their hearts ache and they are exhausted.

164

FUNERAL

Under the surface and over the mind the rush spills into the heart. WHEN THE DIRT IS THROWN AND THE PANIC RUNS IN SCREAMING, TAKE A deep breath and remember they are not there. That flat and empty shell was a casing of a divine creature so magnificent, a body could no longer contain it. A discarded chrysalis you bury or burn to show respect to the journey, to the love and the learning. They are running through fields of emerald grass, marvelling at the shape of things and remembering what it is to be home again and loved to the edges of every universe that ever existed. They are dancing and touching fore-heads to those they reunite with and nothing has been lost. If post cards could come from home, you would be filled with joy if not jealous of the time they are having. They are not lost, they are not ghosts, they are not misplaced, they have not disappeared and no longer exist. Know this as truth.

165

LET ME GO HOME

Please give me strength; she cried out many times. She was kneeling on grass that was faded and not soft, pulling at it crying and begging for home. This place was so hard and flat, so dense with darkness, hate and fear. Violence and confusion were everywhere, and her heart felt heavy.

Breathe child, be still. Feel your heart beat slow, look at your hands, the creases in your hands. Breathe. My strength is yours, be still, be here.

166

DROPLETS

Tears are not weakness in grief, they are the soul's way of saying I love you.

167

HUMAN BEAUTIFUL

You are magnificent even in your human faultiness and stumbling.

168

TODAY

No, you have not failed. There is no place for shame here anymore. But today you might choose to do things differently, with a seeking mind who wants to feel good again.

169

RECIPE

Sometimes the dash of truth makes the lie too hard to resist.

170

THE BATTLE AT TRAUMA GLEN

She ties the sash of red around her waist; the tassels are like the last strands of faith hanging at her hip along with her Grandmother's voice. A pouch is tied to her belt. Her heart is beating fast. The task before her is crushing. She pushes through the bracken and branches the soft murky ground sponges beneath her feet. Finally, the branches thin out, and she can see the cabin clearly in front of her.

HER EYES SCAN ACROSS THE FAMILIAR TRIMMED HEDGE, SUNLIGHT dusting small beams through the leafy branches. The milky yellow porch posts and the duck blue window frames remain picture-perfect; the large french doors are darkened by overhanging ivy and jasmine. The glossy white weatherboard cladding contrasts with the brass frog door knocker; its mouth is stretched too wide with the hammer in the shape of a distended tongue resting on the Lilypad struck plate.

Her stomach acid turns cold and rises in her throat. She takes a deep breath, and as she exhales, her breath turns to fog. The skin on her arms prickles. She glances over her shoulder, and her long dark curly hair is damp now from sweat. The muscles next to her lip twitch on one side as she raises a flat palm to touch her thumb to her forehead then brings it down to her heart. She is ready.

SHE STEPS UP ON THE PORCH BOARDS, AND THE LACK OF NOISE IS jarring. She holds the door handle, and the cool of the metal adds to the chill. The door swings open silently, not even a groan. She feels like she is walking through a hole in a nest.

SHE WALKS INSIDE AND WAITS, LEAVING THE DOOR AJAR. SHE KNOWS HE will arrive soon.

Malevolence incarnate; gnashing and snarling, a malignant beast with trauma dripping from its teeth like an ooze, storms through the doorway.

WELCOME, SHE SAYS, HER FISTS DARING TO TAKE HIM DOWN AND SCREAM her rage, but she knows it will infuse into her skin. She resists with all her might. It is time. Her nostrils flare, and her hands clench.

He whispers to her in a scratchy husky voice.

My little effete, tender and sickly one, abandoned again? Discarded like a tissue, pathetic ruination. I can't believe you've come back for more! What a time we will have you and me.

Burden! He screams at her. The weight of his quip tears at her; she skitters backwards.

Broken!

He spits and snarls the words, the force throwing her against the bench and onto the ground.

She crawls in agony from the whips of his words to the bench.

He stands over her and the stench of him makes her want to reach.

No one wants you.

Your father didn't want you.

Your family didn't want you.

Your friends don't want you.

Interloper! He bellowed.

You will not make old bones.

You are scarred.

Who are you fooling?

Who do you think you are?

What a joke. They feel sorry for you, you wretched girl.

He opens the drawer and pulls a long leather belt, worn and torn.

He slaps it against his thigh, and it makes a thwack sound.
Do you think you are special?
Do you believe what you saw was real?
It's all in that piteous woeful head. He growls.
She flinches, a small split tears her lip and blood flows.
You are unloved and craving like a dirty little beggar. thwack
You will break. Pity pity pity. thwack
Do you remember what you once were? He bawled.

The words are drilling down, down and down into her stomach, nails in her gut; she ignores the pain.

She pulls herself up to the bench; her bloodied lip feels ripped open like an old tent door in a storm. She grabs the cup. She touches her heart and holds her hand over the cup, and tiny pink tendrils run from her fingertips into the tea, and it steeps.

You are loved, she says softly to the liquid.

You are forgiven, she urges in a forced whisper. Her tears fall, and her head feels squeezed like a rung towel.

He whimpers and jumps back; all of the pottery shakes in the cabinets, teacups and beer mugs clink.

Come, she says kindly. She places the small cup on the table.

He tilts his head and looks at her, dropping the belt to the ground.

Come, she says again.

He doesn't object and begrudgingly staggers like a drunkard; he sits at the table, his bursting hairy body barely fitting. He scratches at an invisible itch and reaches for the cup, so dainty in his gristly hand. He sips the sweet drink, a sly eye upon the woman, his bruised and black drooped eyelids closing slowly. He yawns. He hiccups, the cup drops.

Have you poisoned me? He asks in a small voice.

With snapping and squeaking sounds, he yelps and starts to shrink quickly. Golden rays burst from his fur like sunbeams, and his ugliness and body crumble like old cellophane disintegrating, smaller and smaller. He is as tiny as a baby bird. She swiftly picks him up, placing him in the palm of her hand. He is captured—a warm little ball of fluff and scales.

SHE WHISPERS HER SECOND PRAYER OF GRACE, SHE

BLOWS A SWEET breath upon his scaly body. He closes in on himself, his little body spinning and turning. She sings the song.

Very slowly, a wing unfurls from his furry body. His dark muck glitters and shivers into a shimmering band of light. Another wing unwraps, and the summer hue of yellow glints around its tiny body. The elytra reflect light around the room, the same colour as the green of the scribe's eyes.

He opens an eye in surprise. The little wings start to flap and twirl. He folds in on himself, edges form, and angles jut out. He disappears, and in his place sits a large diamond. She places the diamond in the pouch on her hip. A bird sings, how sweet the sound is.

THERE IS NO NEED TO RETURN HERE. SHE UNDERSTANDS THIS NOW. NO longer a prisoner, she walks into the night.

171

COMPANIONS

He has been told men are leaders and mighty. Big and strong and in charge of decision making for people. But the time for hierarchy is coming to an end and must evolve into companion and advocate.

172

GLIMPSES

I must tell you about faith so you can seek it out and hold it tightly, a lighthouse in the ocean. You might be reassured there is more than this because I have glimpsed it.

173

LOVE

They cannot be split from love and must understand the lie they have been told. Hold each other close and look to God as children ready to learn and grow, be courageous and be comforted. The strength is in the surrender, the weakness is believing they ever had control.

174

FREEWILL

It is your choice. It always has been. You can stay. You can go back. You can fight. You can fly or you may disappear for a while. It is okay. But then you can come out again if you want. It will be hard. But call my name and I will be there. Just be sure your heart is open so you may feel my presence.

175

FLOAT

Deceit and grief can hack at identity, shredding it into fragments. What was -will disappear into what feels like a bottomless crevice. Horror. We can sink like a stone or we can float and look to the stars, ask for comfort, ask for calm. Only then can God and those who watch over us with love step into the water to help us float.

176

CHAINS

A power greater than us can step into the fray and calm with mighty authority. Do not give power to anything but love and God, not with your words nor your actions. Nothing in the shadow can destroy you when you are surrendered to a love always intended for you. Liberation is a choice. Dark choices aren't always obvious but they must be stripped back bare so transformation can begin. The hero's journey is a mountain climb and cannot be started successfully with chained hearts.

177

TINY HANDS

The grown-ups are everything when you are small. But all of this changes when the world gets too big and your hands feel tiny. The gravity of it can feel too much. Medicine can heal but it can also break. But you were never meant to carry this alone. God is near. Not the God men create with angry voices and sly smiles. The architect, the bigger. The uniter. The liberator. Once you hold the tangible realisation for yourself it cannot be denied. You can no sooner deny such alchemy than deny the sun and moon.

178

THUNDERSTORM

The dream does not always hold the sunshine, it is a thunderstorm of chaos, agony and cruelty- burning to the hearts layer. Bring the water, put out the flames and take your place as the beautiful child you were always meant to be. You have done all you can. It is time to hold yourself close.

179

THE STEWARD

Peace, understanding and contemplation will be welcomed and respected. Treasure your stewardship and understand the call to service.

180

BANQUET OF THE HEART

Diluting bliss onto screens parading ego steals away the banquet of the heart that waits for you.

181

THOUGHT SEA

Thoughts are impermanent transmissions sent out and bouncing into those around us. There is no separate, there is no divide. We swim in the same ocean of thought, floating in the salty wonder of colourful coral and creatures or sinking into the depths where teeth await and a hungry tide calls. Your stillness and calm witness will help you glide and float, soaring beneath and above. You can fly or you can be pulled down into the deep. Understand what you transmit, and your world will change.

182

ETERNALLY LIVING

I am a bearer of life. We all are. We contain a spark begging to be shared.
FOR WHEN WE STOP BEING AFRAID OF THE DREAM OF DEATH AND REALISE it does not exist; we are no longer a version of ourselves. We cease being the possibly dying and we become the eternally living.

AFTERWORD

You will go on my darling,
    Across the Etheric Seas,
    To sit in grass so beautiful It lasts for eternity.
    The place between awake and sleep,
    The pause in the second hand,
    The sparkle in a newborn baby's eye Where we all go to understand,
    You are beloved and very treasured,
    A note that is part of a mighty song
    There are no endings only beginnings
    But there is story that does go on...

Blessings to your and yours x KB Eliza

ABOUT THE AUTHOR

The year KB Eliza started to write stories was an unusually wet one, with thunder that made her dog shake. As a young child, she loved to escape into the dimension of storytelling and literature. This was also the year she experienced faith, hope, and a strong notion that there may be more beyond our world than we can perceive. A spiritual quest started, the muse for a life of metaphysical enquiry punctuated by chapters of severe illness and the curious debacle of mortality was answered.

Now the full-time Australian writer dedicates her time to simple living and extracting the thoughts and wonders that arrive most days, inspiring prose and heart filled pondering.

www.ingramcontent.com/pod-product-compliance
Lightning Source LLC
Chambersburg PA
CBHW032337300426
44109CB00041B/1128